Family Scribes

Writing Memories for Your Family Tree!

by Linda Jones

ManeLock Communications

Dedication

Geraldine Jones, my mother, captured our stories in black and white photographs and handwritten letters. Robert Jones Jr., my father, did it griot style, with his words. This book is dedicated to them and to my cousins Freddie Shearin, Norvetta Warren, Shirley Munson for their tireless role in keeping our stories going and our legacies alive.

Acknowledgments

Thanking Q Ragsdale for her artistry and to my friends and associates for their images, their writing and their game-playing time. Deeply grateful to my God-Spirit, for the unconditional inspiration.

Imagine being at one of your family reunions where the elders are repeating the same stories of family traditions, superstitions and special moments that they tell every year. Even though you have heard all of the stories before, you are grateful that the elders are still around to tell them. Now, imagine being at future family gatherings without them. Who will continue to tell the stories? Who will keep the tradition alive?

That familiar scenario is what inspired me to produce *Family Scribes: Writing Memories for Your Family Tree!*

Family Scribes is a multi-generational game where relatives and close friends play a part in remembering stories and capturing them in writing! Family Scribes is not a game of competition; it's a memory-stimulating series of timed-writing activities that culminate in storytelling. Everyone who participates wins!

You don't need to have fancy writing skills to play. Just be ready to go where your memory leads you and write about what you remember in your own unique style.

Enjoy playing Family Scribes. It's a fun way to preserve family stories, create legacies and strengthen family ties!

~Linda Jones, creator of Family Scribes

Table of Contents

05

05

05

What you need to play Family Scribes:

Game leader to keep things moving.

GO

Pens & Three ring notebook paper

Folders or binders for the players to collect their stories

A small container to hold strips of paper. (needed for two of the game activities)

Something to keep track of time

Video or audio recorder (Optional)

About Family Scribes

What is the object of Family Scribes?
To inspire family members to remember, write and preserve family and life stories.

What are the contents of Family Scribes?
The game has six timed writing activities and how-to-play instructions.

How do I play?
Players will be asked by game leader to write stories about things they remember and read what they wrote during the read-aloud storytelling session.

The writing exercises are timed to keep things moving, but players do not have to rush their writing. They can write as much as they can at their own pace. Whatever isn't completed during the activity can be done at a later time.

What is the purpose of the example memories?

Each game activity has one or two short memory stories that were provided as examples to stimulate thought. The game leader can decide whether to read the stories to players before they start to write.

What is the read-aloud session?

The read-aloud session happens right after the writing activity and is the time players get to take turns reading their stories to the other players. These sessions--depending on the nature of the stories--often provoke a mix of amusing banter and emotional exchanges.

How long does each of the game activities last?

Most of the Family Scribes activities can be played within one hour, but there are options to play additional rounds, which take more time. The players determine how long they want to continue. The longer they play, the more written memories they generate.

Can people with writing challenges participate?

Time can be set aside during the read-aloud session to give non-writers an opportunity to share their memories orally.

What happens when we play all of the activities?

This is when your creativity kicks in. Family Scribes exists to get your story writing started. Now you have a basis to make up your own memory activities and continue the fun!

Turn your memories into legacies.
Capture them in writing.

Exchanging Memories

This activity involves writing a ten-minute memory about a family member whose name the players will pick at random. This game should be repeated more than once so each player can walk away with a small collection of positive stories written about them by their relatives or close friends.

HOW TO PLAY:

1 Write your name on a small strip of paper and drop in bowl. When all of the papers have been collected, reach back into the bowl and select one of the strips.

2 Do not mention whose name you selected. If it has your name, make another selection.

3 Spend ten minutes writing a special memory about the person whose name you selected. If you don't know the person well, write a positive observation.

4 If you don't know how to begin, start by writing, "I remember ..."

5 Write your name, date and how you are related to the person you wrote about. If you don't finish story, you can complete later.

6 Take turns reading your stories aloud, then give your story as a gift to the person that you wrote about. If you are concerned about your handwriting, you can rewrite later.

7 Repeat at least two more rounds of the writing and read aloud activity. By the end of the activity, each player should have at least three memory stories written about them by other players.

Now add it to your Family Scribes collection!

GAME LEADER INSTRUCTIONS

- Cut enough strips of paper for each player and pass them out so they can write their names.

- Explain the game to the players. Read the example memory story to stimulate ideas.

- Collect the papers with names in a bowl or small container.

- Pass the bowl around again for players to select a name that is not their own.

- Give players ten minutes to write their special memory about the person they picked. Adjust the time if they need to finish writing a sentence or two.

- Remind players to include their name, date and their relationship to the person that they wrote about.

- After the writing exercise, invite players to take turns reading what they wrote to the group of players.

- Remind the players to give their story to the person that they wrote about as a gift.

- Lead at least two more rounds of the activity so that each player will have gifts of three memories that were written about them. Play as many rounds as you want.

- Consider audio or videotaping the read-aloud session.

WHO CAN PLAY:
Ages 10 or older

HOW MANY CAN PLAY:
Best with four or more

WHAT YOU NEED:

Game leader

Pens & Pencils

Writing paper – cut into strips to write names

Bowl or small container to hold strips of paper

Video or audio recorder (Optional)

Fishing with Momma

I remember when I went on a fishing trip with my Mom and three of her best friends. I was about 24 and was the fly on the wall. I giggled and laughed the entire trip at the funny stories my Mom and her friends told--from the serious gossip about the philandering attorney, the cross-dressing preacher, the pill-pushing doctor who they called the quack and the school-principal who was a functional drunk but never missed a day of school and whose students performed above and beyond grade level. We stopped for beer, snacks and fish bait on the way, and soon we were carting tackle boxes, fishing poles, Frito's and beer to a remote part of the lake. While sitting over their fishing poles and fiddling with the lure, these women drank beer, smoked cigarettes, and threw shade at everyone...including me! They noted the irony of my sitting by a tree pretending to read a book when they knew I feared reptiles. We laughed and laughed, and not one fish ventured close that entire day. Although I had no stories to contribute, I felt like a grown woman going fishing with my Momma and her best friends.

Beverly DeBase, daughter

Sweet Sentiments

Players will write a short memory about their favorite childhood candy. They will take turns reading their stories aloud. This activity is particularly engaging when played by different generations.

HOW TO PLAY:

1 Think about the types of candy that you ate during your childhood. Pick your favorite and spend ten minutes writing about it.

2 Do you remember the name of the candy and how much it cost?

3 What did the candy look like?

4 How did the candy taste?

5 Did your favorite candy remind you of certain people or special moments of the past?

6 When your writing time is up, write your name and date on the story then take turns reading your candy memories to the other players.

Now add it to your Family Scribes collection!

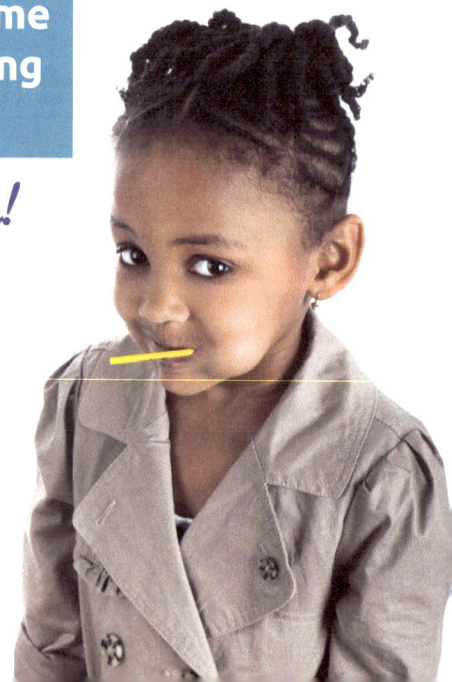

GAME LEADER INSTRUCTIONS

- Explain the game to the players.

- To spark memory, you can read the example story before they write.

- Distribute writing material.

- This activity may make players anxious to talk about their memories before they start writing. Allow brief conversation but remind them that the goal is to have a written memory first. They will have a chance to continue the conversation during the read-aloud session that follows.

- Set the writing time for ten minutes. Allow additional time if they need to complete a sentence or two.

- Begin the read-aloud session by inviting
- players to read their memory stories to the other players. If anyone is shy about reading, offer to read on their behalf.

- Consider videotaping or audio recording the read-aloud session.

My Favorite Candy

Whenever I see Sweet Tarts and Lemonheads on store candy counters, my mind goes back to when I was in fifth grade and they were the new treats on my street. They tasted nothing like the pink bubble gum, licorice sticks, candy cigarettes, Kool-Aid straws, wax lips and Hershey bars that we used to get from the store whenever we had extra change. All of the candy was good, but Sweet Tarts and Lemonheads were better. While those other candies were passively sweet, Sweet Tarts and Lemonheads were boldly sour and they had pucker power!

Biting into those sour candies released a tartness that drew my lips into the shape of a kiss and released just enough sweetness to stretch my pucker into a smile. The Sweet Tarts looked like round, pastel vitamin tablets and Lemonheads looked like tiny yellow candy-covered pearls. I could never eat just one tablet or one little pearl. I had to eat handfuls at a time.

Bill's Grocery is where always had a decent supply of Sweet Tarts and Lemonheads under the glass at the checkout counter. Bill's wasn't a full-service grocery store, but a little mom and pop shop that a carried just enough inventory to tide the neighborhood over over until the adults got paid. Bill's was where Mommie sent me to buy a quarter's worth of 'sweet milk' when we couldn't buy a half-gallon and a stick of butter when we couldn't afford a pound. I don't remember money ever being so tight that she couldn't sometimes press a nickel or dime into my palm to buy some candy--especially my favorites.

Today, decades later, when I see Sweet Tarts and Lemonheads in store candy sections, I will sometimes make a purchase, but since they cost almost two dollars a pack, it is cheaper to simply savor the sour memories of how good they used to taste.

L. Jones

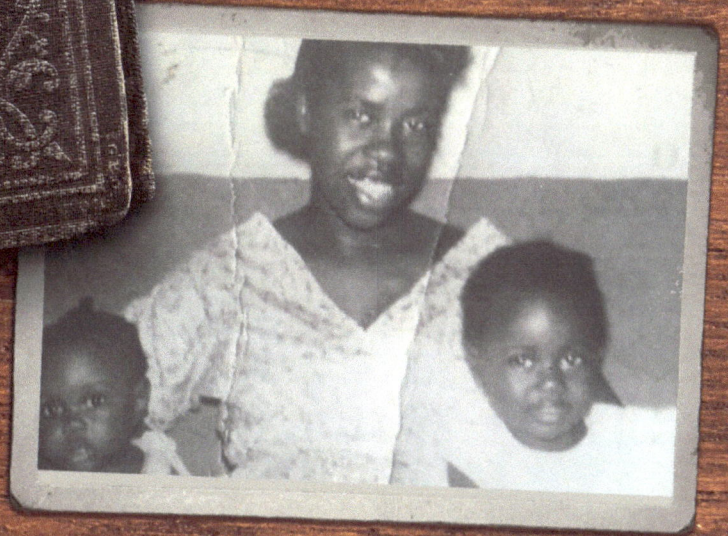

Family Talk and Household Slang

This activity ponders household casual talk--words and language that might be common to family members, but foreign to everyone else!

HOW TO PLAY:

1 Think about the language or words that your family uses and spend ten minutes writing about what you remember.

2 What kind of banter is unique to your household?

3 The game leader can read one of the sample stories to help spark your own thoughts!

4 Be sure to write your name and the date on your finished work.

5 After the writing exercise, take turns reading your story to the other players during the read-aloud session.

6 Enjoy the friendly family banter that these stories often generate.

Now add it to your Family Scribes collection!

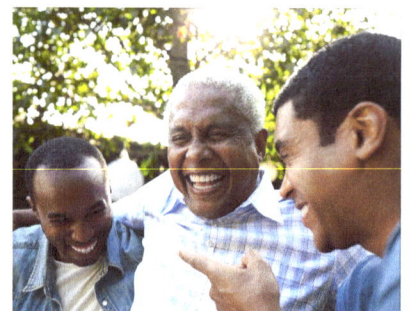

CASUAL CODE

Family members often have their own casual language that may only be understood in their household. Their conversations may be laced with slang of their own creation or words that they mispronounced so often that the right way sounds incorrect. What kind of family slang or colorful code-talk is used in your household now or when you were growing up?

GAME LEADER INSTRUCTIONS

- Make sure everyone has writing materials.

- Explain the writing activity according to the How to Play instructions.

- Read one of the example stories to help stimulate the players' memories.

- Set the writing time for ten minutes. Encourage them to write at their own pace. Allow extra time if they need to finish a thought. They can fully complete their stories later.

- Remind players to put their name and date on their writing.

- Start the read-aloud session by having players take turns reading their stories to the group. Offer to read for those who may be shy.

WHO CAN PLAY:
Ages 12 or older

HOW MANY CAN PLAY:
No limit

WHAT YOU NEED:

Game leader

Pens and writing paper.

Something to keep track of time

My mother's 'flat-form'

"Throw your clothes on the flat-form!" That was the command my mother yelled from the basement to me and my siblings whenever it was time for her to wash our clothes. The 'flat-form' was the landing that marked the halfway point in the stairwell that led to the basement. The 'flat-form' was the wide landing that was about four steps down the stairwell and the place where my mother wanted us to toss our dirty clothes. Tossing them down onto the 'flat-form' saved my mother from having to walk up two flights of stairs to our bedrooms to retrieve our dirty clothes and carry them all the way back down. It was much easier and more responsible for us to meet her halfway. Once she scooped the clothes from the 'flat-form,' she would shove them into the washing machine for a few cycles. After shoving them through the wringer to squeeze out the last drops of water, Mommie would hanging the clothes to dry on the basement clothesline or outside when the weather was nice.

I think I was in high school before it dawned on me that Mommie's 'flat-form' was her spin on the word "platform" although she never intended it to be a variation. According to what she thought she had heard others say, 'flat-form' was the only word she knew to call that landing in the stairwell. We needed no interpretation. When she shouted the command, we knew that it was time for her laundry ritual and knew exactly what to do. I wonder whether our grandmother had a 'flat-form' that was also located halfway down her basement stairwell and whether it was where she commanded my mother and her siblings to toss their dirty clothes? Maybe Grandma actually used the 'right' word but Mommie heard it differently or whether she also used the same spin that she heard from someone else? They are not here to help me trace the word's history, but I am grateful for the memory and for the new appreciation of my mother's innocent vocabulary.

'Slobber sleep'

Slobber sleep was the name that someone in my family gave to the type of deep, ugly, drooling slumber--punctuated with snoring--that we engaged in when we were completely worn out. Unlike the aesthetically respectable surface sleep, "slobber sleep" was so deep that we had no level of consciousness or concern about how we looked or sounded. Slobber sleep was the most restful and restorative state of slumber that I could ever have. I never was able to reach the depths of it in strange places. I could only achieve pure slobber sleep at my home and the purest 'back home' where my people lived. Years ago when one of my sisters detected the stress and anxiety in my voice brought on by my workaholic life the words that she uttered to call me back home to rest needed no interpretation. "Come on home and slobber," she told me. I was on my way.

Experiencing My Name

This activity gives players an opportunity to think of their names as more than just a signature.

HOW TO PLAY:

1 You have had your name all of your life. What has been your experience living with it?

2 Spend ten minutes writing about your name and your 'relationship' with it. What memories are attached to your name?

3 Does it have a special meaning?

4 How do you feel about your name?

5 After you finish writing, don't forget to write the date AND your name!

6 Take turns reading your story to the others during the read-aloud session.

7 Play other rounds of this activity, but this time use different categories like, nickname, preferred name, or middle name!

Now add it to your Family Scribes collection!

Activity 4
Experiencing My Name

GAME LEADER INSTRUCTIONS

• Make sure everyone has writing materials.

• Set the writing time for ten minutes. Allow additional time if players need to complete a thought. They can fully complete their stories later.

• Begin the read-aloud session by inviting players to take turns reading what they wrote.

• Remind players to put their name and date on their writings.

• Consider audio or videotaping the read-aloud session!

• You may lead additional rounds but this time ask about nicknames, middle names, desired names, etc.

WHO CAN PLAY:
Ages 8 or older

HOW MANY CAN PLAY:
No limit

WHAT YOU NEED:

Game leader

Pens and writing paper.

Something to keep track of time

HELLO my name is
Asantewa

HELLO my name is
Greg

HELLO my name is
Dorian

I was born James Dercory Hotzog, after my biological dad who was a Jr. I'm told that my middle name Dercory came from a novel my mom was reading at the time I was born. She didn't remember the title but it was some old romance novel. Whatever book she was reading at the time she would read to me as a baby. She didn't believe in talking baby talk to me. I was born James Dercory Hotzog, after my biological dad who was a Jr. I legally changed my name to Derc Montgomery after my step-dad adopted me. I also did it for singing purposes. People usually stumbled over the name Hotzog. The name Montgomery was just easier for an emcee to introduce me on stage. Sometimes I wish I was still Hotzog. Sometimes a part of me feels like I lost part of my identity. It was a part of me for so long. But I feel that changing it would be very unfair to my son. We're connected by that name. We're carrying on that Montgomery name. I occasionally used Derc Hotzog-Montgomery because a lot of my school friends know me by the old name. Sometimes my original name brings up sadness, but I still love and honor it.

Derc Montgomery

Girl Michael.

My name is Michael. I am a woman, born woman, but I have a name that has historically been given to the male of the species. My father gave it to me, but it is not his name. He gave it to me because he wanted his daughter to have a name that people would remember — something so different that they couldn't forget it easily. It's true. People do remark on it, often. So it probably stays with them. As a young girl, it was awful to have a name usually reserved for the boys in the class. I can remember my teachers asking if I was sure it wasn't Michelle. "Yes," I would say, "I'm sure." Looking back, that was actually a good barometer for how the rest of the school year was going to go.

I have, as an adult, been denied access to my own bank account over the phone even though I could answer all of my own security questions. That was a little frustrating. I wanted my name to be Amy when I was small. Just plain old Amy, a regular old girl's name. It's funny how when you are a child you'd like to be like everyone else. I would have traded that name easily for something else back then. But now, it don't think I'd trade it for anything. It was a gift from both of my parents, and I am grateful to carry their gifts in my name.

Michael Graffeo

Sensory Memories

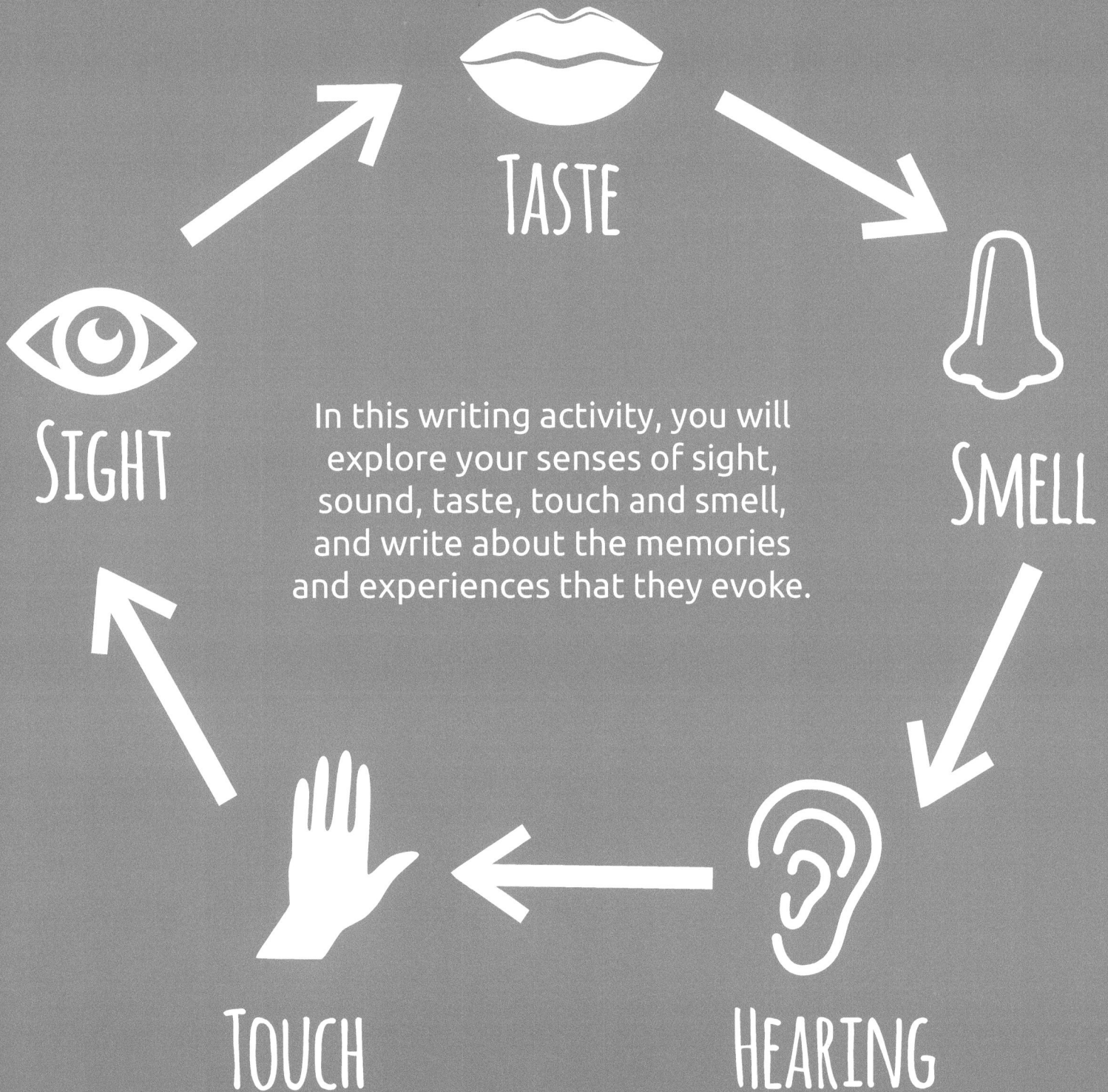

TASTE

SMELL

SIGHT

In this writing activity, you will explore your senses of sight, sound, taste, touch and smell, and write about the memories and experiences that they evoke.

TOUCH

HEARING

HOW TO PLAY:

1 Each player will pick a piece of paper from the game bowl that has one of the five senses written on it.

2 Your senses can help evoke memories from your past. What memories does the sensory word that you picked bring to mind? Spend ten minutes writing about it.

3 When the time is up, take turns reading your sensory memory story to the other players during the read-aloud session.

4 Play several rounds of the activity so you can write memories about different sensory words.

5 Write your name and date on your stories

Now add it to your Family Scribes collection!

NOSTALGIC SENSE

What stories can your senses tell? Your senses might awaken memories about the putrid odor (smell) that emanated from the vacant house on your block or the deafening cheers (sound) of the audience when you won the spelling bee. You might remember the roughness (touch/feel) of the hands of your uncle who was a farmer or the spit shine (sight) that you put on your dress shoes every Sunday before going to church. Do you have memories of the spicy (taste) Indian food that your sister loved to cook but never made enough? What do your senses remember?

GAME LEADER INSTRUCTIONS

- Cut sheet of paper into at least ten strips and label each strip with one of the sensory words: SIGHT - SIGHT - SOUND -TASTE - TOUCH/FEELING - SMELL

- Put the sensory word strips into the game bowl and pass it around so each player can pick one.

- Explain how the game is played and give the players ten minutes to write their memories about their sensory word. Allow more time if they need to finish a sentence or two.

- After the writing exercise, begin the read-aloud session by inviting the players to take turns reading what they wrote.

- If there is a large group and you plan to do several rounds of the activity, save some time by limiting the number of readings in each session.

- Remind players to put their names and the date on their writing.

- Consider audio or videotaping the read-aloud session!

WHO CAN PLAY:
Ages 10 or older

HOW MANY CAN PLAY:
Two or more

WHAT YOU NEED:

Game leader

Pens and writing paper.

Bowl or small container to hold strips of paper

Writing paper – cut into strips to write names

Cookie Monster

Born a cookie monster, I used to eat cookies almost by the jar. My mom really had to stop me when I was a kid, but by the time I was an adult I had learned to pace myself—well, up to a certain point.

In Suriname, we have coconut cookies. Not the coconut drops that you probably know from the Jamaicans. Those are just slides of grated coconut cooked with sugar. Coconut cookies from Suriname were almost like any other cookie that is made with batter. You know, flower, eggs, butter, sugar. and what not, but with grated coconut added to the mix. They are the absolute best! The crunchy sweetness of the cookie flavored with vanilla and mixed with coconut is just delightfully tasty!

In my 30's, when I realized that I had a gluten allergy, I spent the next year looking for replacement cookies. I needed the sugar high. Then slowly but surely, my taste started to change. Without even realizing it, I ate less sugar so I didn't crave much sugar. It is now to a point where every cookie, cake or pastry that I eat has way too much sugar for me. So with that, gone is the cookie monster in me.

Mireille Liong

Sentimental Things

This activity invites players to remember items or places that hold special meaning.

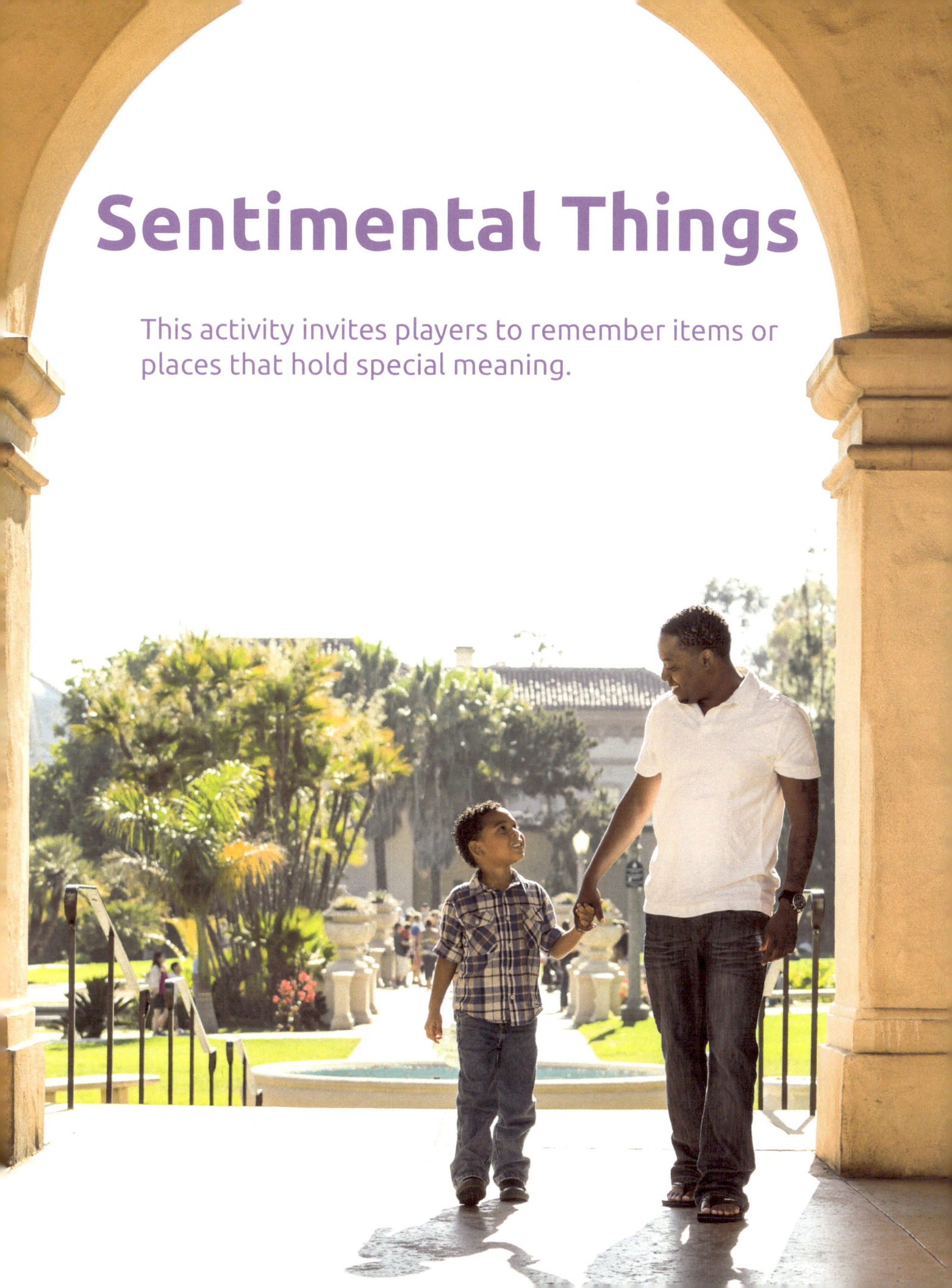

HOW TO PLAY:

1 Think about an item or place with sentimental value. Maybe it's something you own or a special landmark. Maybe it's an elder's walking cane, a certain photograph, a vacant lot near your home.

2 Spend ten minutes writing about the item and the special memories it holds.

3 Be descriptive. Include as many details as possible.

4 If you have trouble getting started, you can always begin with "I remember ... "

5 Be sure to write your name and date when you are done.

6 Take turns reading your memory stories to the other players during the read-aloud session.

7 You can repeat this activity by using categories of other things that might hold sentimental value, i.e. a piece of jewelry, clothing or furniture item, a sentimental toy or a song, etc.

Now add it to your Family Scribes collection!

GAME LEADER INSTRUCTIONS

- Explain the game according to the How to Play instructions.

- Read the Example Memory to players to help provoke thought.

- Set the writing time for ten minutes. Allow additional time if they need it.

- Begin the read-aloud session by inviting players to take turns reading what they wrote.

- Consider videotaping or audio recording the read-aloud session.

- If players are willing, lead them in other rounds of this activity by identifying categories of other things that might hold sentimental value, such as a special piece of jewelry, item of clothing, sentimental song, special toy, furniture item, etc.

HOW MANY CAN PLAY:
No limit

WHAT YOU NEED:

Game leader

Pens and writing paper.

Video or audio recorder
(Optional)

Grandma's piano

Grandma's upright piano, that stately musical instrument that once sat in the living room of her house in Youngstown is what I eventually had moved to my apartment in Detroit after she had passed away. I wanted to have it my space because it connected me to home.

The piano held reminders of that easy going old lady that we visited on our family road trips from Akron during holidays and special occasions. Grandma's house on Regent Street was the magnet for family gatherings and where I could get fresh baked bread and cookies as only authentic grandmothers knew how to make. The upright piano, once adorned with framed 8x10 military and high school photographs of my mother, aunts and uncles, was where Daddy often perched to play a few chords of the "boogie woogie," the only tune that he knew how to play, and it was where Mommie sat to peck for the right key to help her sing-offkey. When I moved the piano to my place, I noticed a 10-year-warranty sticker from the Howard Piano Company, under the lid. The sticker was yellowed and decades past expiration, which made it senseless to contact the company to complain that the piano needed tuning, that one of the white keys got stuck when I played it and one of the black keys rendered no sound at all.

But that didn't matter. I didn't want the piano so it could make music. I wanted it with me for the memories that it played.

                                                                    L. Jones

- Now that you have started capturing your memories in writing, don't stop! Finish some of the stories that you didn't have a chance to complete during the game. You might have a short story in one of them, or an essay in another. One of your memories just might have the makings of a memoir!

- Writing your name and date on your written memories is important. It may not seem like it now but your simple, personal stories may become historic gems for future generations and add branches to the family tree!

- Family Scribes is the game to play at your next family reunion or any gathering of kin and friends!

If you want Family Scribes creator Linda Jones to be the game leader at your next family reunion or other gathering, contact her for details.

linda@thewritingdoula.com
thewritingdoula.com

the
Writing
Doula

Linda Jones, writer, editor and workshop coordinator, provides professional services as The Writing Doula.

Q. Ragsdale provides marketing and business development services as founder of the agency, Orange Moon Media.

Linda's Photo by: Niesha Lanaé Graves
Q's Photo by: Sarah Dergan

www.ingramcontent.com/pod-product-compliance
Lightning Source LLC
LaVergne TN
LVHW072110070426
835509LV00002B/97